Robert Nordstrom

The Sacred Monotony
of Breath

Acknowledgements

Blue Heron Review: "Night Voices," "Sing to the Edge"; *Boston Literary Magazine:* "My Hands Are Full"; *The Comstock Review:* "American Gothic"; *Echoes* and *Echoes Anthology:* "Closet Treasure"; *Families in Society:* "Half-Hour Before Dinner"; *Little Eagle's RE/VERSE:* "At the Dentist," "Good Dog," "Norman Rockwell's Nursing Home Epiphany," "Shifty Meininger," "The Space Between"; *Main Street Rag:* "At the Dentist"; *Miller's Pond:* "Norman Rockwell's Nursing Home Epiphany," "Saved by a Law of Physics"; *Naugatuck River Review:* "One Sided Conversation with My Mechanic"; *Peninsula Pulse:* "Apprehension," "Cracked Vessels," "Drinking Tea Downwind from Auschwitz," "Old Lovers," "Shifty Meininger," "Slippage," "The Space Between"; *Poetry Quarterly:* "Unemployed," "Without His Knowledge or Permission"; *Rosebud:* "Good Dog"; *Staccato Fiction:* "Gridlock"; *Stoneboat Literary Journal:* "Recalling Happy"; *Verse Wisconsin:* "Best Friend—Now an Acquaintance," "Divining the Future While Staring at a Half-Empty Glass on the Kitchen Counter," "Gift or Wish?," "The Healing Side of Glass," "How to Deal with a Midlife Crisis" (online), "Locker Room Gridlock" (online), "Much Rhyme Little Reason"; *Wisconsin Poet's Calendar:* "Campground—Evening—Sault Sainte Marie," "Her Commute"; *Your Daily Poem:* "Closet Treasure," "Half-Hour Before Dinner"

Awards: "Apprehension" and "Cracked Vessels" Honorable Mention in *Peninsula Pulse*'s 2010 Hal Grutzmacher Writers' Expose & Photography Jubilee; "Fish Whispers" Honorable Mention in the 2012 contest; "Old Lovers" First Place and "Slippage" Honorable Mention in the 2014 Hal Prize; "Witness" 2nd Place in the Wisconsin Fellowship of Poets 2013 Triad Contest: Kay Saunders Memorial Award; "Mother's Room—1974-1988" Honorable Mention in the Wisconsin Fellowship of Poets 2014 Triad Contest

The Sacred Monotony
of Breath

Robert Nordstrom

For Linda always. And Eric and Ingrid, a life without whom I cannot imagine and of whom I could not be more proud.

Table of Contents

The Space Between

The hawk understands
in its ascending arc
the weight of the earth
and the attachments she defends

but the sky presents other problems
shifting currents...directionless expanses

like the space between your breasts
or the dreamy glaze of your eyes
as we ride these currents upward
tethered to the occasional posture of desire

to rise but not arrive
to fall but never land
the restless soul reaches for
release that will not come

and so we turn

a slight turn...barely perceptible
and are embraced by
the sacred monotony of breath itself

I

STARTS WITH A DOODLE

Apprehension

A boy stuffs newspapers
into a bag on a front porch.
Remember this moment forever,
the boy challenges himself,
not for the quality of that moment,
but for the possibility of apprehending
the trajectory of his life

then. A half century later
only the collage remains,
stitched images with edges and seams—
mother, long dead, hair in curlers,
nibbling an egg salad sandwich
on the dark side of a screen door;
dog, long dead, napping
beneath the shade of an oak;
robin pecking for worms.

A time capsule with no
message to apprehend,
a bottle tossed back
to the relentless tide

as one
moment dissolves into
another moment
and nothing is
apprehended
then
or
now.

Shifty Meininger

It all starts with a doodle,
always a doodle,
triangles with convex
or concave supports
burdened beneath the weight of
blackened-in circles
whose imperfect circumferences
grow larger and larger
as the hand tries to
steady the mind until
—voila—there's an eye, a nose, or
even, just now, a marble and
—voila again—Shifty Meininger,
the best shot on the playground,
his skinny as a doodle ten-year-old self
leaning back, right foot cut
inward and inching up
to the scratch I scratched
with a stick in the dirt,
left eye shut,
right one squinting
on my prize cat's eye boulder,
holding that shiny silver steely
I've coveted since it spilled out
of his bag delicately between
thumb and finger finger,
and I'm thinking
what kind of fool puts up
his prize cat's eye boulder against
a guy named Shifty
as he slides his hand
forward and back
forward and back and
—voila—lets it fly

true, too true, splitting
my cat's eye right in half
in an odd kind of Sunday School justice
that makes me think of
wise old King Solomon
and how I should have told Shifty
as he was eying up my cat's eye:
Stop, just take it, go on take it,
it's yours.

Saved by a Law of Physics

Just as I Am
pricked my childhood
like a doctor's needle,
corralled my adolescent hormones
into a pen of penitence and doubt
that finally lifted me off the pew
and up the aisle
just as I was
when I was twelve years old.

The man said
just invite Him in and
be cleansed by the Blood
of the Lamb shed for me:
A new boy
bound for glory
born again
this time outside his mother's womb.

What superhero aficionado could resist
such miraculous and transformative power
though he and He and I
did not count on that
Sweet Sweet Jesus
cleavage placed strategically by Satan
two sinners down

or my parent's triumphant smiles
in the car on the way home

or my best friend's plans for a shoplifting orgy
of squirt guns and yo-yos the morning after

or that incontrovertible law of physics stating that
every action requires an equal and measurable reaction.

On the Way to Church

Why was the fat black woman
Sitting and laughing in a puddle of pee
In Kewpee's parking lot
On Sunday morning
On our way to church?
And was it a frown Mother wore?
A scowl?
Was it the nimbus of fear
I saw cloud her face?
I'm not sure. I don't remember.
But I can still feel
Mother's thumb and fingers
Cup my chin and turn me
In the direction she was looking.
I can still feel that Lot-like desire to look back
And the Lot-like fear that prevented me from doing so.
And I still remember the silence
Of Mother's Sunday morning command to forget
The *who what where when why*
Of the fat black woman
Sitting and laughing in a puddle of pee
In Kewpee's parking lot
On Sunday morning
On our way to church.

Best Friend, Now an Acquaintance

At the Mexican border they confiscated
one switchblade but not the other,
which I gave to my childhood
blood brother. Eyes wide and lit
strangely, more pleased with the gift
than I wanted him to be,
he flicked it
open and shut
open and shut.

That's what I remember about
my childhood friend
my best friend then
four decades later
while listening to someone on the radio
bemoan the fate
of the land rover on Mars:
"Spirit's little belly may be resting on a rock,"
he says,
as Spirit's little wheels spin
and Mars's red eye blinks
open and shut
open and shut.

American Gothic

The night I peed out the cabin window
from the top bunk at Camp Miakonda,
my scoutmaster, as pissed off as I was pissed out,
dropped me and my sleeping bag
like a recalcitrant puppy
next to the newly wet upon leaves.
The 1950s—little protection from a scoutmaster
with little patience for a little shit
with the temerity to interrupt his intimate moment
with a Camel at the fire pit.

Or, for that matter, from a clueless mother who
figured her son needed a new kind of scouting experience,
so dropped him like sin
into a Good News Club basement to
sing songs, memorize scriptures,
work through exciting Bible lessons
using colorful materials,
the flyer said.

Don't remember a thing about Good News
other than the bad news of having to go.
Puberty has its own lesson plans:

like peeking out the dining room window,
peanut butter and jelly sandwich in hand,
to watch my older brother seduce
the next door babysitter,

or standing in a dark hallway as Mother
cupped and lifted her naked breasts to the mirror
one night when I got up for a glass of water,

or appraising my Good News den mother's family
in a front row pew at church,
father, mother, unmarried knocked-up daughter
still and straight as pitchforks
in my newly artful eye.

Universe of Adolescence

Last year
she shimmied beneath
the loose garments

of sarcasm and laughter.
This year fabrics tighten
spine stiffens

lush auburn hair
frames hooded eyes
and politic smiles.

Frowning into the hide 'n
seek bathroom mirror
she turns as predictably

as a sun-
seeking planet, exploring
from every azimuth angle

that dark star third-eye
zit winking
beneath a hillock of powder.

Thanks, Coach

During a spittle-spray half-time pep talk
my ninth grade football coach offered the following advice:
When there's a pile up
and you see an opposing player's leg sticking out,
don't step over it, step on it.

Dumb as a platoon of turtles crossing a highway
we nodded—*thanks, coach, that makes perfect sense,*
why bother with Xs and Os when you're wearing
secret weapons on your feet?
then shuffled back out on the field prepared
to tuck up tight as a fetus
the next time we found ourselves at the bottom of the pile.

Google, synonym for procrastination, the roof is leaking
but there's useless information to be gleaned,
I keyed in coach's name, and his obit popped up
like he thought I'd never ask, making me wonder if
this Google-worthy adolescent role model par excellence,

survived by a loving wife, three children and numerous grandchildren,
all-star athlete inducted into his high school's Athletic Hall of Fame,
recipient of a BA, MS, PhD and Distinguished Alumni Award,
university dean, Professor Emeritus, and beloved teacher and coach,

before moving on to serve twenty years in the state legislature
as House Assembly Speaker, Senate Majority Leader—
only legislator to hold the top positions in both Houses—
Senate Hall of Fame inductee, sponsor of
the Ethics in Government Law as well as legislation to fund
veterans cemeteries,

similar to the one in which he now lies—tucked
at the bottom of the pile.

Above the Rim

She peers above the rim of her glasses.
I recognize her immediately.
A bit fleshy, but the same feline eyes,
the high school mascot—a panther—
rising in the rearview mirror
of high school reunion photos posted online.

A couple of decades before David Lynch hijacked
Bobby Vinton's early 60s fashion obsession,
she and I staked out a square foot of real estate
in the high school gym shuffling through
our own blue velvet fantasies:

Sticky flip of hair melting against our cheeks,
bitter strands dipped in Jade East sweat
curling into the corner of our mouths,
newly budded bodies pressing into
Smokey promises of

love...first love...first breast
falling like forbidden fruit into my trembling hand,
tongues exploring territories
only we and the French knew about
electric shivers coursing through the body
as if it were a conduit connecting earth to heaven to...

Who were you? she seems to ask.
Who are you? I seem to respond—
melodrama not so different from that
which saved us from teenage ruin
so many years ago.

My thumb taps time, assassin's finger twitches,
I dip my chin, take one last look above the rim.

Sudden Beauty

The morning mirror
explains everything:

the slick-lipped girls
with their carnivorous smiles,
arms outstretched
like gulls on a downdraft,
swooping in for a quick cheek-to-cheek,
then breaking into loopy illegible signatures,

the boys, backpacks swinging,
banking in pursuit,
crossing her t's dotting her i's,

these extravagant hallways
and grim metal-clad walls
leaning inward,

this gauntlet
through which she glides
like a queen on a float.

Geometry of the American Dream

Back then they called you the product
of a broken, irreparably damaged,
plate thrown against the wall and
shattered, pieces scattered, home.
To me, that meant half perfect,
one less set of parental eyes to deceive:
midnight bike rides down Monroe Street,
trailer court girls with crooked smiles
and raspy voices who might, just might,
you pointed out like a tour guide,
let you cop a feel.
But of course I always hightailed it
before the moon waxed full.
Jumped the creek, crossed the field to
safety on a post-war oak-lined street.
America the Beautiful,
you must have hummed from the other side
as men sporting (or was it sporting men?)
grease-stained t-shirts
stretched over tabletop bellies
knocked on your trailer door
or the blond bug-eyed half-crazy
kid three trailers down
bragged about fucking his sister.
The losers, the losers, the losers,
you always explained, then spit.
But seduction *was* your gift.
When no one was looking, you slipped
beneath the radar of suburban expectations
to tackle the geometry of green lawns
and shimmering sprinklers, the mythic joys
of nuclear families smiling through a nuclear age.
Upward mobility, another proud tick notched
on the American Dream, we cheered

as you clawed your way from neighborhood
to neighborhood, each with greener lawns than the last.
Today we sit on bar stools
twisting our shared history into anecdote.
I remember the romance of danger
I touched but did not inhabit.
You speak wistfully about
seeding, fertilizing, mowing, aeration,
that lawn of dreams beckoning, as it always has,
from the crease of a barmaid's cleavage.
As we must, we part, as we did
so many years ago—
you, now, to your Mercedes, me to my Camry
at opposite ends of the lot.
Looking back, we both agree
the grass could use more rain.

The World We Pretended Then

The summer of my baby does the *Hanky Panky*,
I baked to a sweet potato sheen watching
adolescent heads dip like bobbers in sun-spangled waves,
then pop to the surface to suck the jukebox
filtered air, translucent torsos flailing
in a wild dervish dance
to the titillating lure of hanky
and panky financed on quarters
pilfered from mothers' purses.

My brother not so lucky a few summers earlier,
the summer of *Does Your Chewing Gum Lose It's Flavour
(On the Bedpost Overnight)*, when one dipped
but didn't bob—fisherman's dream
lifeguard's nightmare—and he dove into
the cool quarry depths to retrieve, then kiss
a young man's cool blue lips...

as cool and blue
as those of the summer of *(I Can't Get No) Satisfaction*,
I believe, when he pulled the hearse into the drive
to grab a quick sandwich on the way to the mortuary
and asked if I wanted to see a dead guy—
"Hey, Bob, do you want to see a dead guy?"
was what he said—which of course I did,
of course I did,
so he opened the vault-like Caddy door and
there he was, an old blue man
who once played golf with President Eisenhower
the obit later boasted.

                    Fast forward
to the summer after Jim, Jimmie and Janice died:
highway tie-up on a mail run to Quang Tri,
crowd donning black silk pajamas and paddy hats
gathers around two young men and a young woman,
stripped to the waist and pocked
with small muddy-red holes, staring
heavenward like sightless angels blinded
by the sun those British boys promised was coming.

We looked   we listened
then retreated
from the dirge of snot and tears
dripping onto a gurney of dirt
to retrieve

news from the World
we pretended then
meant home and melodies
that might save us all.

Pledge Drive

and I wanna be
and I wanna be
and I wanna be
~From "I'm On The Outside (Looking In)," Little Anthony and the Imperials

PBS knows how to open a checkbook:
A little *Under the Boardwalk* the pen pops out,
Up on the Roof the decimal point slides over a notch.
And Smokey—play a little Smokey
I'm doing a slow motion grope
in a square foot of floor space
and the chaperones are getting nervous.

But that's when they make their mistake
and take the pocketbook break,
soft shoe it to hosts Leslie & Tom,
a chubby aging bald guy and silver-haired matron
wearing a string of pearls and a cheerleader smile
intimating reverie has its price
and it's time you pay.

The phones ring and the dollar board turns,
stadium perched volunteers in khaki slacks
sporting neatly trimmed beards
pick up and jot down—
"Just a few more callers," Leslie coaxes.
"Boy, doesn't this bring back the memories?" Tom responds.
"Those were the days," Leslie concludes.

I'm getting impatient, the mood is fading.
I think I see Leslie's fingertips touch the back of Tom's hand
as she says, "Can't wait for Little Anthony coming up next."
Tom quivers a shy flirtatious smile,
slides the blessed hand into the safety of his pocket
and I'm gone—back on the inside once again.

II

TOUCH WHAT YOU TRUST

Recognition

he hangs
from memory's slender branch

lets go
grateful for soft leafy soil

throws his last coin
into an empty square
as payment to travel elsewhere

lies
in strange beds
seeking warmth and knowledge
from women whose touch raises questions
like welts on taut perfect flesh

sings songs
to calm the wild speculations
of his children's
own turbulent identities

reads books
tracing the perfectly scribed
lives of others

lies asleep
and is gazed upon by another
who too asks

who am I
as eyes flutter open
to offer in trade

the gift of recognition

Linda Lights a Candle

Even in daylight
she lights the candle

to announce our presence
to the room

to remind us of will
and abeyance

the collapse of Babel's tower
into silence

flame the prayer
air the sacrifice

she will not
waste

Her Commute

Each morning
toast coffee dog

business done
she points due north

toward the old growth pine and clean snow
the precious silence of cold and slow

motion suspended
her life her love her extraordinary

gift of grace pointing
like a flow-chart arrow

toward evergreen land
all exits closed

but one where
inhaling deeply

she braces against
the heroic curve eastward

the gravitas
of the just-risen sun

Without His Knowledge or Permission

the clock stops
digital glitch
fortuitous opportunity
to relive time squandered or catch up with life missed:

dig deeper in the frig for those blueberries hiding
behind a chunk of cheese
take a left turn to let the dog sniff
roadside snacks for one more block
slow down to let the fidgety Ford merge
lift his head off the pillow to tell his wife she looks lovely
in that blazer she irons with her hands in front of the mirror

or skip breakfast
yank the leash
honk the horn
and replay his voyeuristic silence as she slims cloth
over her shapely hips
while fleeing into his freeway future.

He reaches to reset the clock
and for one blue flummoxed moment

                              hangs

like an inert pendulum
awaiting the tick.

Good Dog

My dog's a liar and she isn't very good at it.
Chin resting on her paws, she looks up at me
with her cartoon-cute eyes as if to say—*Who me?*
I have no idea what happened to the cracker.
But I'm not falling for her mendacious ways.
The soup cracker on the table was there
when I left the room and gone
when I returned. She has no alibi,
no sentient ravenous being to blame
so we lapse into a meltdown stare down,
which I know I'll win because she,
like her peers, can't bear confrontation
unless prepared to do something about it—
and she isn't.

I step outside and light a cigarette.
This morning I told my wife I had quit
for good. Looked her dead
in the eyes and said—*that's it.*
She smiled sweetly and gave me
a patronizing pat on the shoulder.

I flip my butt deep into the ferns
and go back inside. Dog lies
in the same spot, cracker
on the floor under the table
not two feet from her quivering nose.
Shameless, I pat her head,
Good dog.

No Question Is a Stupid Question

When I fold the laundry
all her socks and tops are inside out.
I've asked her about this several times

over the past 35 years—"So, Honey,
why is it all your socks and tops are inside out?"—
but don't remember receiving

a satisfactory answer. A question
hardly worth asking,
you are thinking, and I agree,

though I am from the school that teaches
no question is a stupid question.
Please, before I go on to tell you

that I take my socks and tops off right side out,
which I do,
do not dismiss these observations

as one more OCD poet attempting to elevate
the mundane to the sublime—
I never claimed the laundry basket was glowing.

It's just one more observation
become one more fact
begging one more question

from one more basket of laundry,
just something to think about
to keep myself from thinking about

laundry baskets without
all those socks and tops
inside out.

Much Rhyme, Little Reason

The morning tastes sour
Starting off, as we did, dour
Talk of dollars and cents
Who spends what on what we vent
Our opinions on whose debits most worthy
Making us both feel surly
Though as usual me doing most of the talking
And you expressing your opinion by walking
Out the door and into the day
While I go my separate way
To scour a dollar store shelf
Then offer my best self
To a gap-toothed clerk
Who receives the perk
Of my smile and cash
As I walk out with my trash.

Enough

She: "You're self-centered and controlling,
not particularly giving,
but you are good at the core
and I love you very much."

He: "You're manipulative and secretive,
avoid taking a stand that might expose yourself,
but you are always compassionate and kind."

A casual roses and thorns conversation
over a glass of wine, candlelight
illuminating what still burns.
Because of? Or in spite of?
A question set aside long ago
to chase its own tail.

The conversation turns to the mundane
like a flower to the sun.
They blow out the candle and move to the kitchen.
He chops, she stirs. Together
they set the table: fork on the left, knife,
turned inward, spoon on the right.
She lights the candle,
he bows—
the 35-year-old mystery of
his eager gaze and her generous laughter
at a table full of people
they no longer remember
enough.

How to Deal with a Mid-Life Crisis

Forget the tawdry fling with the big-bosomed tart
or the tumultuous affair with the woman who reminds you,
though you don't know it, of the girl you danced your
first slow dance with in junior high
or the raucous nights out with the boys swilling
sentiments as pathetic as the glory stories of a pot-bellied jock
and don't, whatever you do, go to Las Vegas—
they're clichés, all of them, clichés.

No, dig some steps into the side of a hill instead.
Start in early spring before the thaw settles
deeper than the holes you have to dig.
The soil should be rocky with roots
as tangled as your motivations for starting
this masochistic project in the first place.
Take your time, you've got all summer,
but don't let inclement weather stop you.
The steps should not follow the shortest distance
between two points but wind like the curl of the worms
you expose to sudden light.
Set these worms gently to the side
but declare open season on the slugs lying in wait
for the hostas that will eventually garnish
your mid-life masterpiece.

Level the timbers by eye, haul field stone from the old
cow path at the bottom of the hill in the black wheelbarrow
with silver scratches.
Lean into it—thighs clenched, toes digging
into the hill—lean into it.
Pack the gray moss-riddled stone into the side of the hill
dirt congealing the blood on your aching fingers
as your mindless mind wanders over the profound warnings

and encouragements you might place in a time capsule
for another man who might one day push a spade
into this sacred soil.

Keep your eyes on the work and do not
glance up to the top of the hill where the hammock hangs
and your wife and, yes, lover, lounges
one arm draped over the side
a frosty glass of lemonade held in her small hand.
If you feel her bemused gaze, do not imagine it as triumphant,
but for the sake of sympathy it is permissible
to touch the small of your back and grimace slightly.
Take it the proverbial one step at a time,
until one hot summer day you reach the top
to bow, then touch what you trust
with your dirt-encrusted fingers.

John-Boy, Marshal Dillon and My Aging Prostate

There are worse ways to start the day than watching John-Boy's
pursuit of excellence up there on Walton Mountain,
or Marshal Dillon, almost Zen-like in his emotional restraint,
mete out evenhanded justice to the most hardened
and uncivil of outlaws.

Such is the blessing of an aging prostate
nudging a swollen bladder
into a 5 AM wakeup call.

I could turn to CNN to find out what happened in the light
while I rummaged through the night,
but knowing what the Nikkei did would surely spoil the surprise
of what the Dow will do. Besides, at this time of day
at this point in my life I'm more interested in
moral guidance than portfolio prognostications.

Not that I don't have my own advice to offer:
John-Boy, word to the wise:
keep an eye on that blemish on your cheek
but don't have it removed unless...well...you know
it turns on you in your later years.
And Matt—for god's sake, man—Kitty, the woman wants you.
She deserves a little more than small talk over whiskey neat
or dinner for four with Doc and Festus.

Before you know it, it's 7 AM: wife's out of the shower, naked,
looking better than Kitty herself in front of the makeup mirror.
She flips the channel to *Today* and I'm forced to watch
the other Matt describe breaking news carnage
—22 dead, 13 of them kids—
in some unpronounceable part of the world,

then segue seamlessly into Big Al's big toothy smile
and what's happening in my neck of the woods.

What's happening is my leg slipping over the side of the bed,
foot touching the cool wood floor, right arm pushing
the torso into an upright position to greet the day.
What's happening is Bon Jovi preparing to rock my morning
from the square just outside the NBC studios.
What's happening is I flick off the TV and stare at the black screen
announcing finally
the dead are dead
without justice
without opportunity
to pursue excellence—
Today.

Athletes

Father O'Grady flipped the coin
said he was her she was his
teammate. Stiff,
like his collar,
the ardor of locker rooms
and hard-muscled boys
easier to understand
than this noisy train
of tin cans and flashy signs
announcing a new game in town.

        Rookie love—
one sweaty-palmed boy
one eager-eyed girl
gazing heavenward
at a coin tumbling
heads over tails

          over thirty-five zip—
their favor
no meager feat
when one considers
the bookmaker's odds.
They learned quickly
it's not all physical sport.
Sometimes they must lie
together without touching,
stare glassy-eyed at
the soul-chilling countenance
of their opponent.
Then they understand
their love is athletic.
Then they pray
their coin never falls.

My Daughter's Boyfriend's Father Died

He went to California on vacation, they put him in the hospital, and he died. In the hospital, they said he was getting better. His son and wife chatted with him in the morning, then they left the room, then ten minutes later he died.

My wife and I attend the funeral on Saturday morning. That evening we go to a wedding. In between, a friend calls and says he is having a baby.

At the wedding my wife and I dance and dance and dance. A middle-aged woman stands at the corner of the dance floor smiling at us. Her husband sits alone peeling the label off a bottle of beer.

My fingers splay across the familiar curve of my wife's back. I carry her weight as we turn through ballads as humid as the night.

At the funeral my daughter's boyfriend said the night his father died he listened to a song he had heard many times before but didn't recognize the lyrics.

In the car on the way home from the wedding, my wife says "what" but I hadn't said anything.

Harvesting What Remains

Got him back in '93,
the year the nurse called
with the news, then asked for
Dad's corneas.

Runt of the litter, looked like
the progeny of a punk rocker
and ET. All eyes and ears and
ugly as a wart. The kids,
more prescient than I,
said he's the one.
Back home he sat on my foot
like a growth needing attention,
pleased to have escaped
that litter of rude and ravenous siblings.

The night he had a stroke
we carried him upstairs
to our bed, purring over him
the way he purred over us
for fifteen years,
until we slipped off
into our own sunrise assumptions.

In the morning he was gone:.
Thumped his way off the bed and
dragged himself two flights down
to hang his tail over a muddy litter box puddle.
We gathered him up and put him in the car,
held our breath and stared unblinking
into those green inviolate eyes
as the vet inserted the needle.

Waiting for the Kitchen Floor to Dry

One day one of us will dance alone
over this pocked, cracked vinyl.

One day one of us will shuffle
memory's deck for the other
in this bright room of laughter and song.

One day one of us will extend an arm
and be crushed by the weight of absence.

Until then, we surrender to ballads
as lush as a velvet casket,
arms and breasts and legs

floating in Chagallian reverie above two
blood-red glasses of wine.

Old Lovers

Two lovers lie in bed, air thin
between them, ceiling a black cloud
absorbing their dreams.

Their hands touch,
incidental contact,
and in silence they begin

their climb to gain a view,
see where they have been
where they might yet go.

Over there, one says, no,
over there, the other responds,
but neither sees what the other sees.

The cynic says, see, there is no there
there, only breath at whose peaks and valleys
we die and are resurrected again.

Ah, but these old lovers know better,
eyes closed now to open the view, calling
without you I never would have gone there.

III

STRANGE CONVERSATIONS

Lake Sirens

Street side:
weed-scrabble yards
half-dead daisies
pushing through the broken spokes
of an old wooden wagon wheel
rusted out Chevy on blocks—
dirt decoration for big bellied men
crushing beer cans in their fists.
But no one is loitering
in this late afternoon apocalypse.
Sirens draped in white gauze
cigarettes scissored in red-tipped fingers
have lured them away with their lilting

cocktails are served.

They're on the other side now
nails scrubbed pinkies hooked
watching sailboats sink into the setting sun.

Fish Whispers

At home just a half-hour ago
an old man, gait wide and arthritic,
scuttled precariously across a Baghdad street.
The newscaster frowned, as if he knew
something the old man and I did not.

Here,
feet planted solidly in park grass,
I watch a woman wearing a blue shirt
and camouflage hat loop
her bamboo pole toward the sky
then water. She strokes the pole
like a ritual of luck.
Her son, six or so, climbs the rail
and leans parallel to the pole
daring that bobber to move.

The boy, more sky
than water at this stage of life,
does not understand that
luck precludes desire
here. He cocks his head as if
listening to fish whispers
below. Strange conversation:
like adults in the kitchen
just before sleep
or the dance of a bobber
on gray murky water
or the silent sun-drenched descent of dust
in a bombed out building
on the other side of a Baghdad street.

Driving home a squirrel darts beneath my car
but in the mirror lives.

At the Dentist

Stretched out in this space-age La-Z-Boy
a high-speed Swedish-steel factory
whining inside my head
this guy cradles my head against his belly
like maybe he thinks it's *me* who's whining
and tells me *he* had a bad day
Dow Jones dropped 500 plus
but that's not his problem
and even if it were
these high-rise windows don't open
my palms are sweaty
but it's *his* bad day
and *my* bad luck
to be listening to this shit
my whole life it seems
just can't get a word in edgewise
what with this noise inside my head
and these people who make their point
despite the din
leaving me no recourse
but to wish I were a bald toothless monk
with the wisdom to understand
why these two skinny boys
and sullen little fat girl
are hanging in a frame
on a wall
next to a plant noose
in front of a window
that won't open

Friends and Fictions

Our stories evoke howls and hesitancies
squeamish laughter deliciously unkind
denouements sober and just

half-smiles off balance
prepared to turn
one way or the other

at the next delicate rendering.
An honest performance
we congratulate ourselves

though truth be told
we care not whether the truth be told
but only that we may pour forth stories

from the chambers of our oft-vain
occasionally heroic
hearts.

Dear Facebook Friend

Thirty-six Facebook friends wish me happy birthday. Margie, who lived five houses down the block during childhood and adolescence, is particularly gracious, offering, *"Have a great day and wonderful 65th year ahead :)"*—more words than we spoke to each other all through grade school and high school.

I attempt to conjure up Margie the child by staring at her 65-year-old postage stamp visage on the computer screen but am visited instead by a neat line of postwar cape cod cubes, the slip of bedroom window spilling my brave heart into neighborhood secrets on hot summer nights, the jungle gym of new home constructions on whose tightrope rafters I tempted death and foundations I christened with urine, the tangle of trees at the end of the block whose summits offered a view above and out.

Thank you, Margie, for your kind wishes and keyboard smile, but I wonder: did we climb the same tree, search for microscopic life in the same mud puddle, kick the same stone down the blacktop of Rambo Lane? Perhaps—but who will ever know? The question too intimate and I don't know you well enough to ask.

Oh, that shared geographic coordinates were reason enough to celebrate friendship and Facebook not designed primarily for those whose presents are too weighted to ignore, histories too light to trace.

Nevertheless, thank you Margie for your kind and thoughtful birthday greeting and my brief journey into our unshared history.

Bumper Sticker World

LEGALIZE FREEDOM
SUPPORT OUR TROOPS
I'D RATHER BE AT THE CABIN

It's a FORD-TOUGH-in-your-face bumper sticker world.

Back in '71, in The World
one day back from Viet Nam,
I visited the new mall
on the field where a few years earlier
I had honed my soldierly skills
sniping snowballs at passing cars
and watched a couple of young boys
throw coins into a fountain.

Are we the insurgents or their counters?
I asked myself. Depends on which side
of the watershed you're falling,
I supposed.

I cried in the parking lot.
Not sure why.
Spilt milk?
Today, the malls are there when they leave,
there when they return.

There's talk these days of making our new vets
our new GREATEST GENERATION.
A bumper sticker bonanza.
Seems not quite fair to my father
whose ship was sunk on D-Day
but if he were alive I don't think
he'd give a shit. I don't think
our new vets give a shit either.

But we who are born to the slogan
care. Put it on a ballot. Democracy in action—
which is worth more:
DEAD KRAUT or DEAD TOWEL HEAD?
DEAD NIP or DEAD DUNE COON?
And don't forget the GOOKS:
they taught us we must never be afraid
to surge again,

that the malls await our return,
drop a penny in the fountain,
uniform at our feet and go shopping,
maybe some North Woods cabinwear
to slip into when we slip out to
the water's edge, stiff drink in hand,
and empty our pockets
listening to the loon's lament.

Locker Room Gridlock

We're standing there naked.
Ron, at least I think that's his name, tips
on his toes to reach the remote on top
of the locker next to the TV on which our president
who is visiting our city this very moment
talks about unlocking the economy at a lock company.
He clicks off the TV, looks surprised when he turns
and sees me looking up at the now blank screen.
You didn't want to watch? he asks,
though I hear it as a statement,
and I say, *It's better than all the Fox shit
usually blaring,* then quickly add, *I'm a fan.*
I'm hoping my response sounds light and casual,
because I like this guy; he's in his early 70s,
in great shape, smiles quickly and sincerely—
a soft spoken guy of substance has been my impression.
Truth is, though, he took me by surprise and
I'm feeling a bit irritated and now disappointed
that Ron (is that his name?) is more conservative
than I wish him to be. With the TV off,
there's a new silence in the room and it's getting louder.
I towel off and rummage through my locker,
stewing in my own juices now. I'd like to break
this silence, simmer the stew that's bubbling
toward a boil, but all I can picture is our president,
midsentence, assassinated with a remote,
and Ron's surprised but stitched-lip determination
when he turned and saw me standing there naked and staring
at the blank screen. Of course, a few years ago
I might have done the same thing
if GW was up there mangling the language and the world
with his good ole boy *Y'all want another beer while we watch
these bombs blow things up?* But that's the problem,
isn't it? We're all a bunch of cheerleaders and assassins

with remotes. I buckle up, run a comb through the few hairs left
and head for the locker room door.
I don't say anything, no *see ya later* or *have a good day*—
nothing. And more nothing coming from behind me.
I leave the gym with a bad feeling trumping the endorphins
I should be bouncing across the lot with right now.
Almost 65 years old and this is what it's come to:
A couple of naked old farts grappling for the remote,
then filibusters of silence.
Why? The aisle's no wider than a locker room bench—
easily crossed if you're holding the compromise key.
Maybe next time I'll suggest putting the TV on mute.
I'll read as if I'm hearing impaired; he'll salute
when the flag is raised. But when we speak
we *will* hear what the other is saying,
America *will* be blessed.

Gridlock

I stuck a political candidate's sign in my front yard parallel to the street and facing the guy's house across the street. Two days later my neighbor placed his candidate's sign, the one opposed to my candidate, in his front yard perpendicular to my sign. If I'm honest about it, his sign's placement was more to the purpose of political signs in general than mine was because people driving up and down the street could see who he was rooting for, regardless which way they were heading, easier than they could see who I was cheering for. But, ok, I have to admit, I took his sign a little personal. Looking at the two signs from my front window, I felt like his sign was kind of aggressive the way it lined up with my sign; if you were to extend his sign in a direct line across the street, it would pierce my sign like a dagger. So one night when my wife was gone and no one was around outside, I walked into my front yard, pulled the thin metal poles holding my candidate out of the ground, and stuck it in perpendicular to the street like his. It was dark and hard to see, so I had to reposition it a couple of times to get its edge directly in line with his sign. Back inside my house, I wondered what my neighbor would think when he got up in the morning and saw I had changed my sign. I noticed how his sign was placed, so I guess I assumed he'd notice mine, too. He seems like a nice enough guy, but we don't talk much. From my garage the other day, I saw him looking across the street toward my house. I don't know why but I stepped behind my car so he wouldn't see me. *It's the little things*, I thought, as the garage door was shutting, which made me feel sort of uneasy, although I told myself that at least the people driving up and down the street have a choice no matter which way they're headed.

One-Sided Conversation with My Mechanic

I went to the VA last week for an MRI. Took over two hours
'cause the images kept coming out blurry. I forgot to take
my teeth out—the metal, you know—but I didn't say nothin'.
Got a tumor on my toe. They want to give me a prosthesis.
I told them just take the damn thing off—it's only a toe
for Christ's sake. My wife's wrist is still bothering her.
Can you believe it—they put cadaver bones in there.
The slider is bad, whatever the hell that means. I won't let her
ride her Harley; if she hits gravel she can't hold it up.
Business has been slow so I've been cutting thistle
for the county, and now I'm getting backed up. Go figure.
The wife's got these migraines, too, and she got hooked
on pain killers. Took her to the emergency room
a couple of times. One time I had to get a wheelchair
'cause she couldn't get out of the car her head hurt so bad.
The doctor said he shouldn't do it but gave her what he called
a Triple Whammy—one shot, two shot, three shot, and
bingo, the headache was gone. Oh, and we got a pug.
The guy charged me 300 bucks and he's a mess.
Kept in a cage for two years and the grate made his feet curl.
He likes women better than men but he's only bit me once.

First Warm Day of Winter

Windows drop to their terminal crunch.
Stocking hats, gloves, coats
spill onto the filthy floor, fitting punishment for mothers
thinking they might out-forecast a Wisconsin weatherman
on this first warm day of winter.
Nolan and Carter practice their farting noises
as if they're going to be tested on it tomorrow.
Alex yells "hot dogs, hot dogs, get your hot dogs,"
out the window for eight miles straight.
Val tells me she smells dirty feet and they might be hers,
at least I think that's what she's saying
because it's tough to hear over Nathan's
rat-a-tat-tat destruction of every living thing
from his sniper's perch two rows back.
Travis, a fourth grader, launches into an improv
for an eager audience of three kindergarteners:
"I went into a restaurant," he says,
"and they gave me a poop sandwich."
The girls throw their arms in the air,
then collapse against the vinyl seats in squeals of laughter.
In the big mirror he flashes me an *oh, yeah* smile.
The sixth grade girls, sophisticated well beyond such nonsense,
lean into the aisle at the back of the bus,
primo seats for which they have waited six long years,
huddled into dramas as thick as a Shakespearean fog
in which "fair is foul, and foul is fair."
Behind me, Ryan, whom I moved to the front—
his punishment now mine—tells me
he's got this really inappropriate song, *heh, heh,*
stuck in his head, *heh, heh,*
and he can't get it out, *heh, heh.*
"Taylor! Taylor! what do you have on your head?"
"Underwear, underwear, her underwear," the chorus responds.
From her pocket, not her body—I breathe a sigh of relief.

Her brother, suddenly alert, takes notes:
Tomorrow I will receive her, or her parents',
heartfelt apology on wide-lined paper:
I am sory putin underware on my head
mistr B your frend Taylor.
I hit the reds, brake softly.
Doors swoosh open and children wobble down the aisle
like penguins wearing backpacks.
Josh stops at my side to announce, serious as a news anchor,
"My pregnant fish died this morning,"
then contorts his face into a hideous, walleyed grin
and leaps two-footed off the bus.
In the mirror Ava ejects herself
from the back-bus huddle, smile turning to a frown
as the circle closes and locks behind her.
She recovers quickly, jams ear buds in her head,
flashes me a big-mirror holiday smile
and saunters cool as the other side of a pillow down the aisle.
I lean into the window's warm scentless air.
These children, these children, these children—
why do I love them so? Because they open the windows
on the first warm day of winter,
inhabit their stories before parody obscures.

Nothing in Particular Day

Getting to the bottom of it.
Like a kid looking for microscopic life

in a puddle. A biologist the evolutionary prime
on which every thing depends.

A physicist the dark matter behind which
impulse crouches. Out the window

clouds color mood
on a nothing-in-particular day—

mauve trimmed with ash, muddy
palette of malevolence and mercy.

Neighborhood cat loiters
near the bird feeder.

Skittish finch picks a seed,
wings a dip-soar line to the trees.

Shelter, beating heart fearless for food,
he returns

as the paw lifts
and body ripples.

Unemployed

Last night he dreamed he was sitting on a toilet,
no walls, in the middle of the desert.
Men, women and children in bright-colored robes
walked by but did not look.

Awake, he stares at black diamonds on the tile floor
while relieving his dream-swollen bladder.

Questions:
As an infant did he stare at his mother's breasts
wondering which to suckle?
Should he turn on the spigot
or wait for the rains to come?

Answers:
Paralysis occurs when the options are equivalent.
The geraniums can't wait on this blue arid day.

Outside
hose pulsates like a ready-to-burst artery.
Dog lifts her head, eyes following his promise
to point her in life's right direction.

He picks up the ball and throws it as far as he can,
waits for her to show him where it lands.

The Party

You excuse yourself
walk into a room
shut the door
lock's click
signal to review
the things you thought
but did not say
said before you thought
scripted play
looping inside your head:

trenchant rejoinders
righteous ripostes
the witty and whiny
pouring
from your flaccid vessel.

On the other side
laughter and flirtation
cornered conversations
considerations of cleavage
imbroglios filtered
through politic smiles turning
on a dime call

you to your other self
as you open the door
and retake your place.

Gift or Wish?

at the beach
a gull watches
a man bury
his flat-chested wife
in the sand
he gifts her
with large breasts
smooth rosy pebbles
for nipples
the man squats low
to take a picture
precocious gull
watching
yellow
shutterless eye
warning

Weather

Sunning myself on the beach
I watch two lonely figures step gingerly
over ice groaning in the distance.
From here it's hard to hear

over the noisy children building castles
in the sand, waves lapping like puppies
on this blue sunny day. From here,
propped on elbows, sun in my eyes,

it's hard to see who they are,
a man and a woman, I believe,
parkas cinched tight against a bitter wind.
From here, it's hard to know

what they are saying,
these two insular figures huddled together
now, sinking to their knees,
ice breaking up around them,

one weeping, the other laughing
then one laughing, the other weeping
as if to balance the weight
of rogue emotion that might sink them both.

Oh, how quickly weather changes while sunning on the beach.
Oh, how resolute and brave they are.

Campground — Evening — Sault Sainte Marie

Big Wheels with beds and stoves and toilets and showers,
nooks and crannies holding everything needed
to survive the highway wilderness,
plopped down and plugged in along the river.

Terns and gulls chase speedboats chasing
a fat sun slipping into evening's pocket.

The sky darkens and one by one doors open
spilling soft-bellied pilgrims
from aluminum and fiberglass shelters,
sloped shoulders slumped
beneath the burdens of leisure,
dragging lawn chairs to the river's edge.

Fires, untended, behind them now,
they follow the fading light
of starlit freighters inching
toward deeper waters.

Picture or Poem?

Sun at the brink
of its long slow dip into
the Lake Superior drink.

Cumulous mottled sky paints
jigsaw shadows over castles
melting into the sand.

Birch trunks jut from the distant bluffs
like ancient shipwrecks.

Picture or poem?
the question posed in the fading light, though
the important one has already been answered:

what's held is lost,
what's released discovered,

despite the trajectory of a sinking sun
and gull pacing
like a jailor with a watch.

IV

PLEASE REPEAT THAT, PLEASE

Night Voices

In youth
just before sleep
someone whispered
sometimes shouted
but I could not make out
what he sometimes she
was saying. The voice
too soft or too loud
to unravel the clue
unveil the mystery.

Today
brittle memories
prescient messages—
questions turn
rhetorical with age.

Heedless
as I was then
and still am
I keep interrupting—
What...what...what? Please
repeat that please.

Ego

As if saying it well were enough—
unraveling language knots
while lounging on a chaise

nodding yes before off

pirouetting
like a 15-year-old gymnast
dancing in white space

hoping for that perfect 10
and tight-lipped bow
to thunderous applause.

Later I clean the garage—
clean it well—
and for a moment think

that's enough for the headstone:
He kept a clean garage
though maybe in caps, bold,
with a fancy font.

Authenticity

The child understands the cloud is something
he need not name, unlike the small pebbles
digging into his back where he lies.

In bed, staring at the ceiling,
the man sees an old man with a beard
then swirls of plaster...old man...plaster...
and feels shamed by his need for precision.

The man opens a door and enters a room.
A voice, barely audible, whispers,
Again.
Don't make me watch you open the door and enter the room.
Open the door and enter the room
again.

What was the child's prayer before
he was told how to pray?
What did the child understand before
he was told God's plan?

How does the man learn
how to enter a room and shut the door
again?

Articles of Faith

"Mysteries are not to be solved. The eye goes blind when it only wants to see why."
Rumi, "Someone Digging In The Ground"

I would like *the* answer to *the* question.
No, I don't care about *the* question;
I would like *a* question
deserving of *the* answer. In fact
I don't care about *the* answer
but just *an* answer to *a* question.

A question...*an* answer

but with this caveat:
a question that dissolves like *The* Host
on the tongue as *an* answer arises,
that celebrates *the* question within *an* answer,
the answer within *a* question,
that inhabits itself as the child
inhabits himself before he is told
the question he has not yet learned to ask,
the answer he has not yet been told
to believe—

that reveals
the solipsistic secrets
of the yawning years before
settling like soil over his diminished body
and heretical dreams:

question
answer
one.

Drinking Tea Downwind from Auschwitz
(Kazimierz, Krakow)

She sits with tea beneath a tree
near the wall where Jews once wailed
and stylish women now pass over
cobblestone streets
bright colored skirts stiletto heels
fashioning this day's final solution
to the haunting plaints of
mothers fathers children
grandparents uncles aunts neighbors
counted
crated
killed
ashes set adrift in fertile orbits
over fecund fields
the cold stone steps of
empty synagogues
the hungry roots of
a weeping tree
under which she
and tea
untouched
turn cold

Abe's Self-Defense

"... there are two possible situations — one can either do this or that. My honest opinion and my friendly advice is this: do it or do not do it — you will regret both."
Søren Kierkegaard, *Either/Or*

Yahweh spoke
or so Abe claims
instructed gather the wood
raise the knife
above the bound body
of the promised son.

Risky courtroom strategy
perilous defense

but what choice Abe levels
with level gaze *did I have:*
To stay my arm or let it fall—
the birth of faiths
the blessing of peoples and nations
null and void either way

or are murder and mercy
two aspects of His perfect countenance
might the promise broken reveal the promise fulfilled
the unstayed arm deliver abeyance?

Silence.
Yahweh chooses *His* apophatic lessons.
Abe took the leap.

Now   here   on this stand
so like in size and attention
to that cursed altar before which history prostrates
Abe's word of His Word
the only stones left to tilt the scales
he offers himself to his jury of peers:

Retire   deliberate
seek shelter if you must at reason's murky edges
but do not be swayed by the ram that appeared—
not all's well that ends well.

Unspecified Crimes Notwithstanding

Last night I sank three fingers,
the ones Boy Scouts raise
when they promise to help old ladies
cross the street safely,
into an eye socket and dug out
someone's eyeball, an act of violence
more curious than disturbing
hunched over a bowl of bran flakes
and blueberries the morning after.
Friend? Enemy?
A stranger's wrong turn into the wrong dream?
I do not know as my dream, like most dreams,
was heavy on melodrama but light on explication.
Later the same night but different dream
I found myself strapped to a table on death row
waiting to be executed for an unspecified crime
that I did not commit and had little interest in
contesting. My childhood best friend,
whom I last saw a quarter century ago,
leaned over the table and kissed me deeply
and passionately on the mouth. This kiss,
I decided while lying helplessly bound
to table and dream, was reasonable and acceptable.
Heterosexual proclivity notwithstanding,
anyone about to be executed for an unknown crime
he did not commit deserves a moment
of passion with whomever is available
before the lever is yanked, trigger squeezed, or tablet dropped.
Of course, I conveniently awoke in the nick of time,
as we all do, and now find myself sitting at the kitchen table
unbound   reprieved
serving out a Tuesday morning sentence of
fiber and fruit for which I *should* feel grateful.

I'm Sorry

I would like to say I'm sorry,
but to whom? God

has His own mea culpas to sort through.
And if He's not, why should I be?

But I am. And that's *why* I am.
Because I am—

teetering on that Cartesian-Christian precipice
separating first breath from death.

On TV a beautiful brunette,
as serene and alluring as only

the colon-cleansed can be,
scratches a love message to her laxative

in the sand: *I (heart) my lax.* But
when the camera turns

and what was bought now wishes to be sold,
I believe even she picks up her stick to scratch

*I'm sorry, I'm sorry, I'm sorry...*over and over
like a penitent child at the blackboard

until the sun sets and the spring tide rises
to cleanse our slate again.

Divining the Future While Staring at a Half-Empty Glass on the Kitchen Counter

First to go will be the dusting—
no one plays the piano anymore
anyway. The pictures on the wall
will hang askew from many years of
doors banging shut
but I'll hardly notice because
my head tilts just right now
I mean then.
The single bowl on the kitchen counter
can be rinsed quickly when the need arises
and if I lift the edges of the garbage bag
I'll likely be good for another few
tenuously precious days.
Forgive me, these, my housekeeping sins,
I will whisper to the stained carpets
and graying walls
while padding through dim rooms
paper towel and bottle of Windex in hand
opening portholes
to a sea of uncut grass waving
in the cool November breeze.

V

OLD NEWS YELLOWING

Unbidden

Memory abides
to arise

unbidden guest
wrong day

wrong time
call

you don't wish
to answer

door opens
blows quickly shut

a syllable in search
of a word

Closet Treasure

I love those old black & white saw-toothed Kodak moments:
the confusing scowl in a sea of smiles,
the mysterious sidelong glance
that didn't make the photo album cut,

the ones mothers frowned at while shuffling
through the stack a couple of weeks after the family picnic
then dropped into the unmarked grave
of a cardboard box,

but kept, like chipped china,
their Instamatic truth safe
from Photoshop crop, or worse,
the digital click into oblivion.

Remembering Mother After She Lost Her Memory and Almost Took Mine with Her

Folding newspapers on the front porch
three slaps and a tuck   three slaps and a tuck

mother, hair in curlers,
a shadow in a house dress lifting
Love Is a Many Splendored Thing
to the blank wall above the piano.

Ten years later
she's walking down Rambo Lane,
curling iron in hand, cursing
as Dad coaxes her
like a cat into a cage
into the car

where I sit spinning childhood's wheel:
Cheerios mornings and PBJ afternoons,
soprano trill laughter
punctuated with a Juicy Fruit snap,
her tears, my laughter
when the yard stick breaks,
the heading here then there
in the back seat of the old Ford.

And now,
fall breeze lifting leaves
off the big oak in the front yard,
her memory mine,

a shade in a housedress
suffused in a soap opera's blue glow
old news yellowing
on the porches of strangers.

The Old Rocker

The old Windsor sits empty but has held many.
Its moon-sliver rockers have worn welts in rugs
and ridges into the grainy surfaces of maple and oak.
Bow-tied men wearing seersucker suits,
women decked out in baubles and frills,
infants suckled and soothed into their drowsy futures
have all tested the mettle of this chair.

When a boy came calling on my daughter,
I liked to sit him in that chair.
Did he lean into the room anxious
to eject himself from its polished hollows?
Or did he settle against the sack-back spindles,
hands resting comfortably on the burnished walnut paddles,
in easy communion with all those who have settled here
before him?

This chair evaluates character
like an old man sitting in a dark corner
whom everyone thinks is fast asleep.
It's the last chair left
for the last person standing
in a crowded room
who doesn't know
how honored he is.

Mother's Room—1974-1988

1.
when the body remains   curls
like a fetus seeking return

the loved one prays
to ceramic angels scattered throughout the room

2.
when the body remains   roots
like a weed that cannot be pulled

the loved one tills
soil where daisies fail to bloom

3.
when the body remains   wears
the ring but abdicates the throne

the loved one whispers
secrets to assassins who respond no...wait...soon

4.
when the body remains   when the body remains
the room consumes what the heart can no longer sustain

The Night Before the First Day

sitting on the edge of the bed
in his son's old room,
the one he moves into when
his wife moves out of
the room they shared for 40-plus years
and a big black demon dog
fangs bared bars his reentry,

a bespectacled old man
scratches his cotton belly
with thick grimed fingers
fingers that avoid the white enamel
of refrigerators and stoves
fumble helplessly
over the tiny knot
of a child's balloon,

mumbling, yes, a demon dog.

He bends to remove his socks,
folds each twice, halves then quarters,
and places them neatly inside his shoes
whose toes he lines up evenly at the foot of the bed.

Yes, a demon dog,
he speaks to the eggshell walls,
so they, too, might comprehend
these new rhythms
that will get him into and out of bed,
to bathroom, kitchen, a bowl of bran flakes
at the table with the pad of paper

covered with doodles
dense enough black enough
to befuddle an exorcist,

then off to the nursing home,
the first day of approximately
5200 to follow,
to touch the hollow cheek
of the woman who surrendered
their room to a demon dog,
cup her muted face
in his newly gentle hands.

Dialing for Dollars

The psychic said you headed for New Orleans
after you left this earthly plane.
I laughed. Not *at* you, Dad,
in case you were tuned into the psychic chatter,
it's just I can't picture you hanging out on Bourbon Street.

You were the guy home from the factory (4:10 sharp)
slipping off the shoes and on the slippers,
sitting in Grandpa's old hand-me-down dusty gray chair,
legs crossed, brow furrowed,
cleaning your comb with a matchbook cover.

I was the one lying on the floor
trading school-day dramas
for Busby Berkeley fantasies
on Dialing for Dollars.

But I kept my eye on you too:

those thick stubby grease-lined fingers,
the heroic thumbnail split by a punch press—
hands that gripped slick oily steel,
pinched your trousers into a little apron
with forefingers and thumbs and
scuttled off to the bathroom to brush off
when Mom called out (4:30 sharp)

dinner's ready

how we prayed and ate and argued
on schedule and in time for you to slip
off the slippers, on the shoes and leave the house (6:30 sharp)
for your evening stint at the machine shop.

No, forgive me for laughing, Dad.
I assumed everything and knew nothing.
Maybe New Orleans
or some extravagant place like it
was exactly what you were dreaming about
as those little flakes flicked
like tiny stars onto your lap.
Maybe you were sneaking a peak
at Dialing for Dollars, too.

Slippage

1.
This morning I drove my mother-in-law to the doctor.
She told me, slow down, not so fast, she needed more time
to think things through—*It's been a long time since
I've been on a job interview.*
When we walked through the door, she whispered,
Where are the typewriters?

2.
Last night I watched Alfred Hitchcock
being interviewed on an old Dick Cavett rerun.
Heavy lidded eyes, pouty lower lip, avuncular belly
on which his meaty hands lay knotted like a bow—
Mr. Hitchcock's wit as delightfully dry as a cool desert night,
Dick's boyish hesitancies and self-aggrandizing puns
as irritating now as they were back then when
I, too, had hair to spare.
I felt that increasingly familiar Leave It to Beaver itch,
a dislocation of time in space,
not nostalgia, but slippage,
a matter of degree.

3.
Upon returning to the nursing home,
my mother-in-law tugged at my arm and said,
*I'm glad I didn't get the job.
I like working here—
I hope they didn't hire someone else
while I was gone.*

4.
One time, while sitting with my mother-in-law
in the nursing home dining room, she said,
These people would rather fall out of their chair
than make any sense.

Sitting at my kitchen table I think,
Tomorrow morning, like this morning,
I will have blueberries and bran flakes.
Or will it be bran flakes and blueberries?

5.
(Note to self [1]: Language becomes meaninglessly interrogative
before becoming refreshingly declarative with age.)

6.
(Note to self [2]: On my next visit I must remember to tell her
I like working here, too.)

Norman Rockwell's Nursing Home Epiphany
(the painting not painted)

There's Charlie
Henry
Frank
pulled up pushed in
to the TV gates
yellow pillow-head hair
electric in the flickering light
watching Weather Channel tornadoes
race across the Midwest—

and there's the nurses and aides
in their blue scrubs and pink smocks
sorting pills and chores
the grandchildren nephews nieces
staring in open mouthed nonplussed
amazement at
Charlie
Henry
Frank
slumped
heads bobbing and weaving
like broken down stallions
whose races have been run

and Norman
who painted the happiness
he did not know how to live
there's Norman
alone in the corner
lower right
partially hidden
by the fern's green fingers
his own elongated finger raised

and pointing—
he may be pointing
we wish him to be pointing—
to the narrow window
where a single amber leaf
falls through splendent light

Their Reason to Celebrate

On their father's eightieth birthday, one son came from
Milwaukee, the other from Tulsa to Toledo to celebrate.
His wife had Alzheimer's disease, for fifteen years, since
the year he bucked his load like a mule who'd had enough
and headed for Ornskoldsvik.

Retired...Sweden—
one month in the old world
for forty-five indentured years in the new one.

Where new gets old fast:
he got a Great Depression, job, wife, world war, two sons,
a long plane ride, some smoked salmon, reindeer, moose
on *tunnbröd* with his brothers and sister who were now
gray, like him, and strangers. They averted their gaze
when his wife came to dinner with her wig on backwards.

So back to the new world to start a new life.
"What are you going to do?" he told his sons, "you never know,
just never know, just what God's will will be."
Every day for fifteen years he slipped his tattooed arm
(a heart split by an arrow) around his wife's shoulders,
rubbed his knuckles against her sunken cheek,
and whispered, *"my bride, my bride."*
She curled on the bed like fruit drying around its pit.

His sons did not see this. Perhaps they sensed it
one night when they peeked in on their own sleeping sons
and saw their own restless history as their reason to celebrate
him.

So they threw a party,
the first one for him anyone could remember.

Cracked Vessels
~For Jayne

All the names and relationships:
husband, brothers, sister,
grandchildren, nephews, nieces;
and the more obscure ones
that make us furrow our brows
and squint to remember for you.
Thank you, you say,
you're very kind to me, you smile
softly with just a tinge of irony
seeping through
the fissures and cracks
illuminating your history
and ours
to reassure us
once again
as you always have
that it's all right
don't worry
don't trouble yourself
in the waning light
you hold for me
in your own
cracked vessels.

Witness

Journey to the end to recall the beginning:
picking at scabs—what do you do
with that brown crusty stuff?

From the birth of Grandfather to the death of me
150 years approximately,

times 10: King Arthur sets the stage
for a 20th century musical,
times 13: we're standing at Golgotha
weeping or selling souvenirs,
times 333: eyes engage,
mouths form syllables that raise an other's brow.

Time chases its tail
language sails two dimensional seas
as the noose-like ratio of year lived to years lived
tightens—

velocity slows
the passage of time speeds forward
Einstein's theory in reverse—

the entire muddled history of humankind
negotiable when personalized
as any aged pilgrim touching those smooth colorless scars
in the dim light of the door's jam
will attest.

VI

WHEN ALL THE PIECES FIT

Sing to the Edge

Stand at the edge and

    sing
to the forest's
black airless pockets

    sing
to the worm-rotted trees bowing
beneath the luxurious silence of new shade

    sing
from the heart Zorba's song
until birds dance in the trees

    sing
until the heavy fruit falls
into streams and rivers

    sing
as their pits roll like stones onto distant shores
to be cupped and kissed by children

    sing
as their black soulless eyes are relit
and sour breath sweetened

    sing
    sing
    sing

to the edge of every thing

A Half-Hour Before Dinner

He runs red-faced
stumbling up the stairs
plants himself solidly
next to my chair
and pauses...
to catch his breath
observe the scene
desk, lamp, bills
even at seven
he understands
that the universe
whether sun, moon, planets
or the lines on his father's face
must me configured in certain ways
to negotiate a cookie
a half-hour before dinner.

To say, sure,
reach deep into that jar
of cold formed earth
and retrieve your prize
hold it high
like a general's flag
behold its dark chips
as the possibility
of pleasure and victory
over immovable forces

or

No! Dinner!
Remember the dinner!
where battles have been waged
and lost,
brussels sprouts, broccoli,
good soldiers of the good earth,
left pierced, broken,
rotting in the field.

I feel him studying me.
No, not me,
this universe parallel to his.
The sweepstakes entry form
lies at the corner of the desk
(who knows, if the stars
are aligned just right).
I crush it in my hand.
Get two, I say,
one for me
and one for you.

The Healing Side of Glass

I catch my reflection in storefront glass
when I pass just as the glass
absorbs the light just right
and I see through myself to the other side
where the naked mannequins stand,
steel rods pushed up their ass,
disjointed arms and legs
awaiting physicians of fashion
to heal their gestures of distress
in dress of mood and mockery.
Do not, like Alice,
I tell myself then,
look too deeply into the glass.
Turn, adjust your focus to new light
on the street, others beside you—
find their pace,
invite their gaze,
make your gesture their balm,
not their malaise.

The Cliff's Edge

Just as I got used to thinking billions
instead of millions, they're telling me
I need to be thinking trillions instead of billions
if I wish to avoid those awkward gaffes
when I confuse my billions and trillions
during mind boggling debt and deficit conversations.

But I'm seldom corrected, which leads me to believe
most everyone else is confusing their trillions
and billions. In fact, some of my more wizened peers,
fingers clutching the cliff's edge,
can't make the leap from millions to billions
let alone trillions.

It's a generational thing. When I was a kid
you could slip a quarter and a nickel
into a cigarette machine and get back three pennies
attached to a pack of Luckies. Today, pennies
float like flotsam in small dishes
next to toothpicks and pricey after-dinner mints,
the free matches gone the way
of fewer Luckies to light.

Oh, those warm summer nights as a kid,
adults encouraging me to count
stars in the sky, hedge against running out of cows
jumping the moon, I suppose.
Today I hear there are 100 sextillion stars in the universe,
though only 400 billion (thank you God for that)
in the Milky Way, reason enough
to lower my gaze,
resume the search for something
precious and new
under the sun.

My Hands Are Full

My hands are full:
28 years of Ohio, 1 Viet Nam,
2 Florida, 1 Paris, 33 Wisconsin,
1 wife, 2 kids, 3 houses, 7 jobs,
3 cats, 4 dogs, 8 cars—
I've arrived, finally, here, in a park,
counting 18 geese, 39 goslings, 8 fishermen
while balancing coffee, donut, lottery ticket
in a slant of early May sunlight.

I will not wait till the end to tell you
that I scratch my ticket and am a $20 winner.
This poem is not about fortune;
it's about arrival, here, a place
never imagined but always known,
where I sip coffee, bite a donut, scratch a ticket,

resisting that tug to tally
what's won,
what's lost.

Recalling Happy

A woman in the coffee shop sitting at the table next to mine
says to her friend, "Tell me about a time when you were happy,
truly happy." I stare at newsprint
straining to hear her friend's response:
not forthcoming and I'm not surprised—
the query too intimate, the response too complex,
to regurgitate on cue while masticating a bagel.
But I'm sitting alone, swimming through bad news
all black and white, and have no excuse.
So I retrieve the marked files: marriage, births of children,
sloppy-tongued puppy with a bow around its neck
running into my arms when I was eight years old.
To no avail—these days such memories feel more like
digits in a sum than highlights of a life.
I'm beginning to feel bad about my failure to recall happy
when the woman's friend throws me a bone:
"When all the pieces fit," she says softly but firmly,
"nothing stands in relief."
I smile and take a bite of bagel,
recalling, for every good reason,
the clematis on the trellis outside my bedroom window,
how it grows a couple of inches overnight this time of year,
the waving fronds of the Japanese iris cheering it on.
Sheer exultation on those full moon nights
I sleep right through.

Made in the USA
Middletown, DE
02 September 2020

16072465R00070